Is It a Day for Work or Play?

Mary Elizabeth Salzmann

Consulting Editor, Diane Craig, M.A./Reading Specialist

Published by ABDO Publishing Company, 4940 Viking Drive, Edina, Minnesota 55435.

Copyright © 2007 by Abdo Consulting Group, Inc. International copyrights reserved in all countries.

No part of this book may be reproduced in any form without written permission from the publisher. SandCastle™ is a trademark and logo of ABDO Publishing Company.

Printed in the United States.

Credits
Edited by: Pam Price
Curriculum Coordinator: Nancy Tuminelly
Cover and Interior Design and Production: Mighty Media
Photo Credits: BananaStock Ltd., Comstock, Corbis Images, Image100, Image Source, ShutterStock, TongRo Image Stock, Wewerka Photography

Library of Congress Cataloging-in-Publication Data
Salzmann, Mary Elizabeth, 1968-
  Is it a day for work or play? / Mary Elizabeth Salzmann.
    p. cm. -- (Antonyms)
  ISBN-13: 978-1-59928-718-8
  ISBN-10: 1-59928-718-8
  1. English language--Synonyms and antonyms--Juvenile literature. I. Title.

PE1591.S266 2007
428.1--dc22
                              2006032023

SandCastle™ books are created by a professional team of educators, reading specialists, and content developers around five essential components—phonemic awareness, phonics, vocabulary, text comprehension, and fluency—to assist young readers as they develop reading skills and strategies and increase their general knowledge. All books are written, reviewed, and leveled for guided reading, early reading intervention, and Accelerated Reader® programs for use in shared, guided, and independent reading and writing activities to support a balanced approach to literacy instruction.

Let Us Know

SandCastle would like to hear your stories about reading this book. What is your favorite page? Was there something hard that you needed help with? Share the ups and downs of learning to read. We want to hear from you! To get posted on the ABDO Publishing Company Web site, send us e-mail at:

sandcastle@abdopublishing.com

SandCastle Level: Transitional

Antonyms are words that have opposite meanings.

Here is a good way to remember what an antonym is:

antonym

=

opposite

Also, **antonym** and **opposite** both start with vowels.

3

antonyms

Sarah is working hard in school.

antonyms

Matthew and Brandon are playing outside.

antonyms

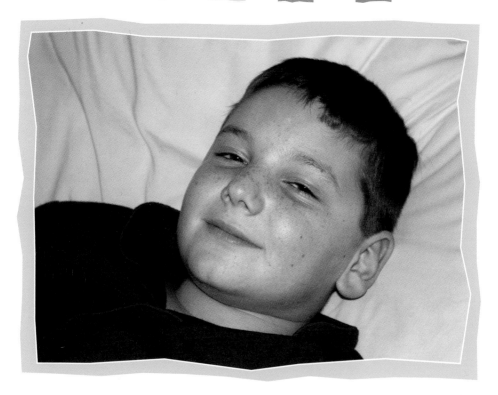

Josh is awake.

antonyms

Abigail is asleep.

antonyms

Grace sits to use the computer.

antonyms

Nicholas stands when he reads aloud to the class.

antonyms

Anthony and Lauren's dad is tall.

antonyms

Jessie's younger brother is short.

11

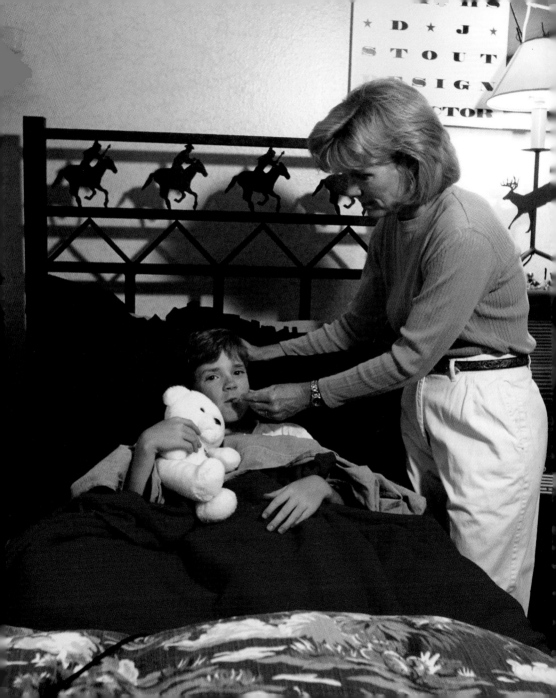

antonyms

Tyler is sick. His mom will give him medicine until he is well.

antonyms

Brianna is Hayden's sister. Hayden is Brianna's brother.

antonyms

Zachary is a child. His dad is an adult. They have fun at the park.

antonyms

Kayla is a girl. Dylan is a boy.
They like to read together.

Antonym Activity

asleep   awake

play   work

boy   girl

sit   stand

Antonym Pairs

adult — child

asleep — awake

boy — girl

brother — sister

play — work

short — tall

sick — well

sit — stand

In each box on page 20, choose the antonym that describes the picture.

Words I Know

Nouns
A noun is a person, place, or thing.

adult, 17

boy, 19

brother, 11, 15

child, 17

class, 9

computer, 8

dad, 10, 17

fun, 17

girl, 19

medicine, 13

mom, 13

park, 17

school, 4

sister, 15

Adjectives
An adjective describes something.

asleep, 7

awake, 6

his, 13, 17

short, 11

sick, 13

tall, 10

well, 13

younger, 11

Words I Know

Verbs
A verb is an action or being word.

are, 5
give, 13
have, 17
is, 4, 6, 7, 10, 11, 13, 15, 17, 19

like, 19
playing, 5
read(s), 9, 19
sits, 8
stands, 9

use, 8
will, 13
working, 4

Proper Nouns
A proper noun is the name of a person, place, or thing.

Abigail, 7
Anthony, 10
Brandon, 5
Brianna, 15
Dylan, 19
Grace, 8

Hayden, 15
Jessie, 11
Josh, 6
Kayla, 19
Lauren, 10
Matthew, 5

Nicholas, 9
Sarah, 4
Tyler, 13
Zachary, 17

About SandCastle™

A professional team of educators, reading specialists, and content developers created the SandCastle™ series to support young readers as they develop reading skills and strategies and increase their general knowledge. The SandCastle™ series has four levels that correspond to early literacy development in young children. The levels are provided to help teachers and parents select appropriate books for young readers.

Emerging Readers
(no flags)

Beginning Readers
(1 flag)

Transitional Readers
(2 flags)

Fluent Readers
(3 flags)

These levels are meant only as a guide. All levels are subject to change.

To see a complete list of SandCastle™ books and other nonfiction titles from ABDO Publishing Company, visit www.abdopublishing.com or contact us at:
4940 Viking Drive, Edina, Minnesota 55435 • 1-800-800-1312 • fax: 1-952-831-1632